C000006198

Fractal Publishing,
Stroud,
Gloucestershire.
Email: fractalpublishing@hotmail.co.uk
Tel: 07961 838304

The poems of Effie M.Roberts
were first published in two volumes,
Winter Jasmine and *The Golden Glory has Fled*,
from Fractal Publishing.
Please contact us for more information.

British Library Cataloguing in Publication Data.
A cataloguing record for this book is available
from the British Library.

ISBN   0-9549622-2-2
ISBN   978-0-9549622-2-7

Printed by Severnprint Limited,
Ashville Industrial Estate, Bristol Rd.
Gloucester. GL2 5EU.
01452 300158.

CONTENTS

THE EDITOR

Philippa Roberts is the granddaughter of
E.M.Roberts. She also grew up in Cheltenham and is
a professional writer who has published short stories,
poetry, book reviews and journalism, at intervals,
over a period of about twenty years. Her work has
appeared in a wide range of publications,
from children's magazines, *Horizon* and *Aquila*,
to *Cadenza* and *Quality Women's Fiction*. It has also
appeared in a number of anthologies.

Her web site, www.modernfairytales.co.uk contains
samples of her published work and samples from her
e-books, which were published in beautiful editions
by *Bowbridge Publishing,* in Stroud, Gloucestershire.
The full manuscript of the poetry journal was also
published as an e-book by Bowbridge. This is sadly
no longer available.

*Warning: There is a pirate version of Effie M.Roberts'
poems being sold over the Internet by a print on demand
company called 'Writers' World'. Its production and
distribution has never been authorised. The book, entitled A
Woman in Wartime, is very shoddy with numerous mistakes
in it, and the family of Effie M.Roberts have, of course,
received none of the profits from the sales.
Please do not buy it.*

INTRODUCTION

Effie Roberts was born, Effie Lawrence, in Sheffield, in 1896. She later moved to Cheltenham with her family, and they lived at the police house in Charlton Kings, where her father was the local policeman. After this they moved to a larger house, Exleigh, off Copt Elm Rd, where she lived until her marriage. She trained as a seamstress during this time, working at Cavendish House in Cheltenham. War first began to cast its shadow over her life when her fiance was killed in action in World War 1.

In a poem in the journal she tells how she eventually 'walked out with' and married his best friend, Charles Roberts, who had admired her courage during the months of grief which had followed her fiance's death. Charles had also fought in WW1 and another poem in the journal tells the story of how a football dropped from the skies brought him the news that the war was over.

Life was still not easy for the young couple after their marriage. Effie had two miscarriages and a still-born girl before their two sons were born. However they did love each other very deeply and the strength of their bond is apparent throughout the journal. Of the boys, the elder was my father, Alan, and the younger, his brother, Clifford. Many of the poems in the journal are about these boys and the experience of bringing them up in wartime.

Effie began the journal in November 1941, when the family was living in Tewkesbury Road, Cheltenham, and the realities of everyday life were very grim.
She had very mixed feelings about her own gift. Women, particularly women of her class did not write poetry, but the impulse to do so was irresistible. Her family loved her writing, and their support helped her.

The world described in her poems is quite alien to the one we live in now. She recreates very vividly the difficulty of groping for her own front door during a blackout, and of having to manage without paper bags when shopping, because shops weren't allowed to give them out when paper was rationed. She wrote about waiting for the coal man to come, about the mouse that got in the oven, and about trying to prepare for Christmas without the foods she would have liked.

She also wrote about her husband and children, describing the evenings that she spent playing the piano and singing, as Charles dozed in his chair. (She never seems quite convinced by his explanation that it is for love of the music!) Her piano was a joy above almost any other, and her musical ear is strongly apparent in the poetry too.

She looked back with great nostalgia to the life she had as a young girl growing up in Sheffield. This was intensified by the fact that she wasn't able to travel to see her family and friends there throughout the war years. When she did return it was to find much of it reduced to rubble.

Many poems tell of the rationing, the queues, the sheer dreariness of their lives during the war, but she never loses her sense of humour. Only occasionally does the sheer bleakness of it all break through. Perhaps one of the most striking instances of this is in the poem that begins,

Last night, I could not sleep,
I lay in bed, and my eyes would keep
Watching the ceiling o'er my bed,
Watching the wet patch spread and spread; -

The stanza concludes

Outside the rain tumbled down.

Each stanza brings a variation on this line, but each one concludes that the rain is still, relentlessly, tumbling down. The rain is a powerful symbol of the war weariness that pervades everything. The poem conveys astonishment at the sheer relentlessness of it, because she was still young enough at this time to be astonished, but the repetition speaks a sadder truth, which she is coming to recognise. Her journey, in spite of this, is a very spiritual journey and she does find her own truth.

The journal ends in 1947 when her husband dies suddenly of a coronary thrombosis. She never recovered from this blow, and never had the confidence, or strength, to write poetry again, although she lived on for another forty years.

Philippa Roberts

SILENT AND STILL IS THE NIGHT

Silent and still is the night,
Stars in their myriads gleam,
Not a stir of a leaf is heard,
All seems so peaceful, serene.

The bustle and tear of the day,
Has ceased for a short, brief spell;
But searchlights sweeping the skies,
Tell us that all is not well;

That there is no peace on earth,
'Tis not so heav'nly as seems;
Perhaps e'er an hour has passed,
We'll all be waked from our dreams.

All through the hours of darkness,
These netted brilliant gleams
Seek for dangers lurking there,
To catch in their dazzling beams.

Soldiers of this battery,
Their ceaseless vigil keep;
For enemy planes they're searching,
Searching the skies while we sleep.

I'VE BEEN FOR MY NEW RATION BOOKS

I've been for my new ration books,
And stood long, awaiting my claim,
I went early to avoid the crush,
And most everyone did the same.

I studied the faces around me,
Some happy, some gloomy and blue,
But may it be said no one grumbled
At having to wait in a queue.

And now I have collected them,
(It's the 'Pink-uns', you know which I mean),
I may go to the shop which I fancy,
And order, just like a queen.

A tin of salmon, or a tin of soup,
A tin of beans in gravy,
Perhaps meat roll and sardines too,
Hurrah for our wonderful navy!

QUEUES

Well, well, I do declare,
Queues, queues everywhere,
Up the High Street and the Strand,
On the pavement, people stand;
Queues, queues at all the shops,
For fruit, fish, biscuits, lollipops,
Cakes and buns, and 'meaty' pies,
　-　Anything to appetise　-
Kettles, saucepans, heaven knows what,
　-　Such is the housewife's happy lot; -
　-　And if for an hour, you patiently wait,
How annoying to be told 'too late;'
When you've as much as you can carry,
And must not any longer tarry,
You take your place in a queue for the bus, -
For a long long time it has been thus: -
But this is the life we live today,
And it's no use grumbling, anyway!

SUCH A FUNNY THING HAPPENED

Such a funny thing happened,
When I was out walking one day,
A man driving a horse and cart,
Was coming along my way.

That horse was trotting along
At just a nice, steady gait,
But this didn't please his master,
He wanted a much quicker rate.

So he raised his whip in fury,
And beat it with such a will,
But that horse, instead of speeding,
Just looked and then stood still!

That man, his face got fiery red,
His temper got worse and worse,
He raved and yelled and shouted,
And heavens, but didn't he curse!

Of course a crowd collected,
As is usual, at a scene,
Man or horse - which would win? -
To see we were all very keen!

Then somehow, - I don't know how, -
What think you we saw there?
That man was sprawling on the ground,
His legs up in the air!

Did we laugh? I'll say we did!
('Twas wicked of us, of course)
That man was duly punished,
For whipping that poor horse.

And when at last he rose,
He looked a trifle shamed,
And yes, he had been punished,
For he was slightly lamed!

SIXTY BEAUTIFUL GOLDFISH

Sixty beautiful goldfish
Lived happily in a pond,
Skimming along the surface,
Or resting beneath a frond.

Of this happy family,
I've a story to relate,
It will grieve you, I know, to learn
The sad end of fifty eight.

A hungry out-sized otter,
Prowling along in the dark,
Hunting for his supper,
Found his way to the park.

'Oh my, oh me, what luck!' says he,
'Oh what a scrumptious feast',
And helped himself to all but two,
The greedy little beast!

Now, was he too fat to hurry,
Or still gloating o'er his feed?
- I cannot say, - but the dangers
Of the road, he did not heed.

A motor car in passing,
Struck the unfortunate otter,
And that, dear reader, was the end,
Of a greedy little rotter!

'TIS LONG SINCE WE HEARD THE CHURCH BELLS CHIME

'Tis long since we heard the church bells chime,
Filling the air with musical rhyme, -
In silence they'll hang in the belfry tower,
Until they proclaim the triumphant hour.

'Tis long since we saw the gaily lit shops,
When evening falls, then the black-out drops;
And we leave the town with so little bought, -
And only the comfort of home is sought.

'Tis long, since we walked with confident gait,
When the lights go down, we leave it to fate; -
Plunged into darkness, we grope around,
And sigh with relief, when our door is found.

'OHO!' LAUGHED THE HEDGEHOG, 'I'VE HAD SUCH FUN...

'Oho!' laughed the hedgehog, 'I've had such fun
Tonight, while out on my usual run
I came across an inquisitive cat,
I believe she thought me a glorified rat!
A curious creature, no doubt, she found me,
She stopped and looked, and then walked round me,
"How strange," she murmured, "What can it be?
And fancy, it isn't afraid of me!"
I set that silly young cat a poser,
Was I a meal? – or –(coming closer),
Something to play with, something to maul,
So I curled up my prickles and curled in a ball! –
You should have heard that young puss howl!
I laughed and went on with my evening prowl.'

MORE RESTRICTIONS! WHAT A JOKE

More restrictions! What a joke,
The nation must save paper, folk; -
That is the order, anyway,
So take your bag, when you shop, today.

Just fancy strolling down the Strand,
With Sunday's joint held in your hand!
It's no use talking nice and sweet, -
The butcher cannot wrap your meat.

Your grocer too, - you'll cause a flutter,
If you've no bag to carry your butter;
Your eggs and cheese, your sugar and tea; -
You see how awkward it's going to be.

Should you forget, then that's a shame,
For you have only yourself to blame,
So at the traders, do not nag,
But always remember to carry your bag!

WHAT DO YOU THINK I'VE DONE?

What do you think I've done?
The silliest thing to be sure,
I washed a pound of currants,
Then spilt them on the floor!
Now who will help to pick them up?
They're rationed, I'll get no more; -
I'll have to wash them all again,
After they've been on the floor:
They're like the sands of the desert, -
To collect a long time 'twill take,
But I *must* have all those currants
To make a Christmas cake.

WHAT A STATE OF CHAOS

What a state of chaos
The world is in today;
Two more countries are at war,
Japan and the U.S.A.

And so another war begins
On Sunday again, you see,
This, the fourth in succession,
It's all very puzzling to me.

First, Germany with Britain,
And think back, the Great War too;
Then Germany with Russia,
Once more this is too true.

Does it seem strange we go to Church
On Sunday, to pray for peace,
And humbly ask of our dear Lord,
That all these conflicts cease?

I find it most disturbing,
Then shades of doubt come stealing; -
Judge not, if at times it brings
Disquiet and ill-feeling.

DOODLE-OO

'How do you do?'
Says doodle-oo,
Determined to be heard,
At morning light,
And dead of night,
You'll hear that noisy bird!

When all is still,
The air he'll fill
With that shrill high-pitched crow,
Why won't he cease,
And keep the peace,
Until the morning's glow?!

He's feathers gay,
A 'cocky' way,
A healthy comb, - oh hec, -
He may be fine
But were he mine,
I'd ring his blessed neck!

But not for long,
You'll hear his song,
For sure, he is a winner;
He hasn't starved,
He'll soon be carved
For someone's Christmas dinner!

So let him glut,
And let him strut,
And crow out all his glory;
He doesn't know
What we all know,
He's near the end of his story!

YOW-OW! GOODNESS! WHAT WAS THAT

Yow-ow! Goodness! What was that
Sending my heart all pit-a-pit pat?
Sitting alone in the firelight's gleam,
A scurrying sound, shatters my dream,
And hurriedly from my chair do I rise,
But nothing I see, so can only surmise
A mouse, in the stillness and dim evening light,
Mistakes the hour, for the darkness of night
And ventures abroad in the quest of a meal –
- Its object in life is to pilfer and steal; -
P'raps I unconsciously stirred in my chair,
And sent the thief scampering off in a scare.

DO YOU REALISE CHRISTMAS IS NEAR?

Do you realise Christmas is near?
I'm afraid there'll be but little of cheer;
It just seems a farce when hearts are sore
And war's destruction lies right at our door;
Still I suppose we must see it through
And say yet again, "A merry Christmas to you."

I guess you are hoping that I will make
A nice rich spicy and iced Christmas cake,
Well, there will be a cake of some sort, it's true
Of currants and raisins, I have just a few;
But icing! - dear me, you may look aghast, -
But icing sugar's a thing of the past!

A Christmas pudding, with brandy sauce! -
Really good people, - I'd love to, of course, -
But that's disappeared, along with the whisky,
There's nothing this year to make you feel frisky;
But we'll be thankful for what we can get,
Even though the fare's plain, we haven't starved yet.

CHRISTMAS BRINGS BACK MEMORIES

Christmas brings back memories,
As I sit in my chair and dream,
My mind goes back, just nineteen years,
Such happy years they've been.

No, I think back one year more,
Thoughts of a former sweetheart
Come surging up within me,
But death caused us to part.

I attended the funeral,
As did also, his boy friend,
After the service we said 'Goodbye'
I thought that was the end.

I never thought to meet him again,
But 'fate' had willed it so,
We met the following Christmas, -
He told me he loved me, you know.

The first time we went out together,
Was to Church on Christmas Eve,
And a black cat sat upon my lap,
With ne'er a 'By your leave'.

As we sang the age-old carols,
It stood between us two,
And purred away so lustily,
This isn't fiction, - it's true.

When we sat down, this blackest of cats,
Curled up, and slept on my knee,
And 'fate' seemed to tell me that night,
That here was the lover for me.

And so it has proved to be,
I courted that boyfriend,
We married two years later,
So this tale has a happy end.

THE DAYS GET LONGER

The days get longer,
The sun grows stronger,
The butterfly's on the wing;
Down the country lane,
I'll soon walk again,
Welcome, thrice welcome is spring.

I saw a daisy,
You'll think me crazy
To shout about such a thing,
But each petal unfurled,
Just tells the whole world,
It's spring again, it's spring.

The song of the thrush! –
Listen, - oh hush! –
He's whistling to the sky,
He welcomes with mirth,
The spring at its birth,
Goodbye, grey winter, goodbye.

The meadow and lea,
Are beckoning me,
The river side is fair,
And my heart is light,
As a bird in flight,
When spring is in the air.

HERE'S AN OLD DIARY FOR '39

Here's an old diary for '39,
I'll sit down and scan these writings of mine, -
What did I do? – Now let me see, -
Ha! Here is something that interests me!

*　　*　　*

Sheffield! – now that makes me restless again, -
I'd love to be off in that north-bound train,
To haunt the markets as of old,
But they're not there now, so I'm told.
I think of friends, and walks spent together,
Tramping the moorlands rich with heather,
Climbing the crags and grassy hills,
Or picnicking by the woodland rills; -
And I'll go again, though I don't know when,
For it's a troubled world, - but until then,
Well, it's nice to reminisce in my chair,
And live once again, the days I spent there.

*　　*　　*

Bought an apple tree from a famous store,
It cost me sixpence, not a penny more, -
It has flourished and grown, and today, right now,
Clustering blossoms adorn every bough.

*　　*　　*

Turning the pages backward, I note,
At Easter-tide I bought a new coat, -
I guess I would want to look rather swell,
So must have bought a new hat as well.

*　　*　　*

Further back still, on Boxing Day morn,
We saw John Peel with his hounds and horn
A colourful scene, with his coat so gay,
A striking contrast on a winter's day; -
From the 'Queens' came the maids, with dignified grace,
In dresses of scarlet and aprons of lace, -
And for each huntsman, a glass of port,
And the toast of course, 'a good day's sport.'

*   *   *

It's an awful day, such blackness and rain,
But on through my book, I'll travel again,
This glimpse in the past is refreshing to me,
I recapture those days by the river and sea.

*   *   *

Tewkesbury, Gloucester in the month of May,
A day by the river, down Evesham way,
Worcester, Stratford, Weston-Super-Mare,
And Cleethorpes! – I quite forgot we spent a day there! –
Barry Island, *that* day was so warm,
But ended with a terrific storm,
The thunder! The lightning! The deluge of rain!
Who cared?! – 'Twas time to get the homeward train.

*   *   *

Went shopping, got wedged in a crowd up town,
Returned without buying that new summer gown,
And made a vow (which I broke so soon,)
To stay at home on Saturday afternoon.

*   *   *

Now here is an evening spent at the fair,
I think we met almost everyone there,
Magnetically drawn to each stall and side show,
With a 'try your skill' cry, or 'come have a go!'
Hoping a token to win as a prize,
A doll or a bear of enormous out-size,
You try your luck, - it's the fun of the fair, -
But your 'tanner' won't stay on that lucky square!

There's chair-planes, the whip (both new 'try-outs')
The mystery ghost train, and round-a-bouts,
Trinkets for presents, and well stocked stalls,
With ginger snap, candy and sweet brandy balls;
Hoop-la's and skittles and coconut shies,
Swings that will carry you near to the skies,
Shooting range, dodge-ums, darts and skee-ball, -
If you've money to spend there's something for all.

There's something about the glitter and glare,
That calls one and all to the fun of the fair.

*   *   *

Weston a second time! Well, well, well!
And Barry too! – We sure did it swell; -
What happy days, so carefree and gay,
Seems but a dream now, - they're so far away:
I saw the gypsy at Barry, and – well, -
She gazed in the crystal, my future to tell,
Property, - money, I would get,
But it hasn't come true, at least, - not yet!

*   *   *

September the third, - here entries cease,
For war came upon us and shattered our peace.

SHALL I FORGET? NO, NEVER, -

Shall I forget? No, never, -
That delightful tree-lined lane,
The beeches with their gnarled roots,
The oaks tall, haughty and vain;
And further on, the view beyond,
Fold upon fold, the hills –
The grass so green, the poppies red,
The daisies' snow white frills:
The tea at the wayside inn
As the pangs of hunger creep,
 - And down below, the sombre woods, -
Have they a secret to keep?

So near to the blue of heaven,
So far from the bustling throng,
Only the coo of the dove
And the blackbird's latest song.
The peace, the charm, the grandeur!
Shall I forget it? – Never!
The beautiful Cotswold countryside,
Will live in my heart for ever.

HULLO,' SAID THE LEAF, WITH LIGHT HEARTED GLEE

'Hullo,' said the leaf, with light hearted glee,
Don't you wish you could tumble about, like me?
I frisk and I frolic, and dance here and there,
It's fun to tumble and roll in the air!
Far away o'er the housetops I fly
Nodding my greetings to friends passing by,
Up and up, o'er the highest church steeple,
Then acrobat down to the feet of the people.
P'raps when I'm tired, down the river I'll float,
Along the side of a barge or a boat,
But for the present, I'm out for a spree,
So goodbye, little puss, you can't follow me!

LAST NIGHT, I *COULD* NOT SLEEP

Last night, I *could* not sleep,
I lay in bed, and my eyes would keep
Watching the ceiling o'er my bed,
Watching the wet patch spread and spread; -
Outside the rain tumbled down.

Hours and hours, -
The whole night through, -
The wind, it whistled and shrieked and blew,
Shattering windows, slamming doors,
Stripping roof tops, flooding floors; -
As the rain came tumbling down.

At last, my weary eyelids closed,
(It seemed but half an hour I dozed) –
And after a night, fantastic, weird,
The first pale streak of dawn appeared; -
But still the rain tumbled down!

The wind has shed its malicious mask, -
But as I perform each daily task,
Sadly I gaze through my window pane,
Wonder if e'er 'twill be fine again –
For the rain still tumbles down!

OH, THE JOY OF APRIL

Oh, the joy of April,
With springtime in the air,
The chorus of the song birds
And nature budding fair;
The daffodils and tulips
Wafting in the breeze,
All the trees and hedgerows
Unfolding their green leaves.

The fruit trees burst with glory,
Lambs frisk about the fields;
The ploughing and the sowing,
That bring the harvest yields:
Oh, the joy of April
When life begins anew!
The dark days are behind us,
We've seen the winter through!

FIVE INCHES OF WATER, OH DEAR ME

Five inches of water, oh dear me,
Scarcely enough to drown a flea -
That's all we must have, so we've been told
When we have a bath- (hot or cold).
My boys I implore you, please, oh please
Don't get VERY dirty knees!

Five inches of water - just fancy that.
How does one manage if big and fat?
A bath a month may be their lot,
Twenty inches, - and piping hot!
The bliss, the joy of an hour well spent,
To wallow and dream to their heart's content!

THE DAY IS ALMOST AT A CLOSE

The day is almost at a close,
'Tis the hour 'tween supper and rest,
I loll at ease in my chair
'Tis the hour that I love best.

The children are tucked up cosy,
Tired, after school and play,
Fast asleep in slumber town,
Dreaming the hours away.

My dear one and I are alone,
Sometimes we will read a book,
Sometimes we talk of the past,
Or perhaps, to the future we look.

But whatever we may do,
Our love will never wane,
'Tis the hour that I love best,
For we are sweethearts again.

O, HEAVENS ABOVE, WHAT NEXT!

O, heavens above, what next!
Now we are rationed with soap!
With washing, bathing, and the rest,
How do you think we will cope?

Such a good excuse I will have,
When I don't want to scrub the floor,
For now I'll be able to say,
'Of soap I've really no more.'

Wouldn't you boys be happy,
If I said 'No wash tonight'?
No matter how black you were,
Your faces would beam so bright.

But my dears, that won't happen,
For some soap I have in store,
So I can't truthfully say,
'Of soap I've really no more.'

WHAT CAN BE THE MATTER WITH ME?

What can be the matter with me?
I'm in the mood of despair.
There is nothing to make me so,
For I haven't a load of care!

I ought to be very happy,
I really am – but you know,
A change from the daily routine
Is a tonic – it bucks you so!

I would love to go to Sheffield,
I would love a ride in a train,
I'd love to visit the old haunts,
Of my native town again.

I would have to spend a week
Once again, with my own folk,
It is three years since we met,
And to me, it is no joke!

I'd like a ride on the trams,
Just two pennies would take me miles,
Right to the tops of those hills,
And blow the cobwebs off the tiles!

I'd like a walk on the moors,
And gather the purple heather,
As I did in years gone by,
A crowd of friends together.

I'd walk across the Bole hills,
Right down to the Rivelin Valley;
To the cottage by the mill wheel;
Across the bridge I'd sally.

And there, I would rest awhile,
And enjoy a cup of tea,
I'd gaze out on the scenery,
So rugged and lovely to see.

A holiday there would make me,
As happy as cows in clover,
But I won't be able to go,
Till this cursed war is over.

HOW REMARKABLY CLEAN ARE THE STREETS

How remarkably clean are the streets,
To waste paper, it now is a crime,
You can be severely punished,
You may even get 'sent down the line'.

There's no more litter in the street,
No paper whirling around,
And don't throw away that ticket,
For nothing must be found.

That empty carton of yours,
Did you put it in the bin?
It's just a scrap of paper,
For why kick up such a din?

Shall I tell you the reason?
I'm sure I have your permission;
Every wee bit is wanted,
To send 'Jerry' to perdition.

So save all your scraps of paper,
To make bullets for the guns,
Bus tickets also, every one,
They are wanted for the Huns!

WHATEVER WAS THAT NOISE?

Whatever was that noise?
I fancy it was a bomb,
Yes the sirens are wailing,
It has shocked us, every one.

We've had a heavenly peace,
For oh, such a long, long time,
It made us go quite goosey,
When we heard the sirens whine.

Our fighters are guarding the skies,
And hark, the roar of guns!
Shrapnel flying all around,
Oh curse the heathenish Huns!

Dad is away on fire-watch,
While we are taking cover,
Away from the bursting shells,
Anxious for one another.

         *   *   *

The danger now is over,
Gone has the signal, 'All clear,'
Many been killed and injured, -
Pray the end of wars be near.

AFTER SO MANY MONTHS OF WAR

After so many months of war,
And the ruins around, we see,
We think – must everything be lost?
And what will the end ever be?

War has left thousands homeless,
And robbed us of many a thing;
Though havoc is left near and far,
It can't take away everything.

We must have the cheerless black-out,
We must have the great guns booming,
But the birds still carol gaily,
And the flowers still keep on blooming.

We still have the leafy woodland,
There is joy in the sunlit hill,
In the breezes, softly sighing,
And the river that's never still.

There is joy in the starlit sky,
And the health-giving sun's warm ray,
We find, when we just think awhile,
There's lots the war can't take away.

IN A SHOP WINDOW UP TOWN

In a shop window, up town,
Sat a mouse, not caring a rap,
Nibbling away at sultanas,
A cheeky and bold little chap.

So utterly regardless
Of attraction that he caused,
He gaily went on munching,
And never once he paused.

He just glanced at passers-by,
With his tiny beady eyes;
Sultanas clasped so tightly,
He looked so wondrous wise.

A wee and cute little creature,
And so outrageously fat,
I thought as I watched him nibbling,
Fancy running away from that!

ALL THE WORLD IS PRAYING FOR YOU

All the world is praying for you,
You wonderful people of Malta;
Bombed incessantly night and day,
Never once does your courage falter.

When peace comes to us once again,
And the horrors of war be gone,
Your gallantry heroic,
In history will ever live on.

Reward will surely come to you,
For outstanding courage, supreme;
Freedom will be yours in the end,
And the past seem an ugly dream.

All the world is praying for you,
Yes, praying upon bended knees,
Have faith, these prayers will be answered,
You'll be freed once again, Maltese.

LISTEN, MY BOYS, AND I'LL TELL YOU

Listen, my boys, and I'll tell you,
Of a tale Daddy told to me
'Twas years ago, in the first war,
And Daddy, a soldier was he.

Three years he spent in the trenches,
Oh such a long weary time,
And he with others were marching,
Once more, right into the line.

Resting awhile by the wayside,
They saw a plane sweep so low,
What was it doing, they wondered?
'Twas British, I'll let you know.

A football was dropped from that plane,
And it bounced back ever so high,
Up and down, till at last it settled,
By the men on the ground near by.

And then what a rush was made,
Now why had that ball been dropped?
They found a note attached to it,
To say that fighting was stopped.

And that was the way Daddy heard
That the armistice had been signed,
The news had made them so happy,
The horrors were now left behind.

And many happy hours they spent,
With that ball dropped from the skies,
While awaiting their orders,
For each to demobilise.

WHY HAS FATE BEEN SO UNKIND?

Why has Fate been so unkind,
To send us this wretched day?
Wind and cold torrential rain,
Has spoiled this Bank Hoiday.

What was the use of planning
A walk in the countryside,
A picnic in the coppice,
Or even a nice bus ride?

Too wet to go to the circus,
Too wet to go to the fair,
Too wet to go to the pictures,
Too wet to go anywhere!

There is nothing else to do
But put all these thoughts aside,
So we'll settle cosily down,
And stay by our own fireside.

What now?! – Something has happened,
To break the monotonous day,
Looking through the window we see,
Two barrage balloons blown away.

Upwards and onwards they go,
Tossed angrily by the gale,
Now they are dipping earthward,
Then skyward again they sail.

They are almost out of sight,
Travelling eastward, on and on;
Where will they land, we wonder?
We see them no more, they're gone!

And now the evening shadows fall,
Still heavily comes the rain,
Tomorrow, when ev'ryone's at work,
The sun will shine bright again!

OH, FOR A SMELL OF THE SEA

Oh, for a smell of the sea,
Oh, for a breath of sea air,
Oh, for a stroll on the sands,
At Weston-Super-Mare.

It is quite three long years,
Since we had a holiday,
'Twould make us very happy,
Could we spend but just a day.

We like to see the children,
Building castles in the sand;
'Tis grand to stroll on the pier,
And listen to all the band.

We'd love to sit on the beach,
(It is not much we crave,)
And watch the in-rushing tide,
Till our feet, its waters lave.

No wish to go on a steamer,
Content to remain on shore;
But we are asked not to travel,
Till this blessed war is o'er.

I'VE STILL ANOTHER RATION BOOK

I've still another ration book,
This time it is for sweets;
We must surrender coupons now,
For nearly all our 'eats'.

No need to stand in any queue,
There's lots of sweets in the shops,
But I must take my ration book,
If I wish to buy lollipops.

Sweets or chocolate – which I like,
From the two I may have my pick,
Two ounces must last me a week,
Well, there's no fear of being sick!

*   *   *

The ration has now been increased,
Only one ounce extra, it's true;
But for small mercies, I'm grateful,
Three ounces is better than two!
For sweets I have such a passion,
So thanks for a larger ration.

MY BOOK OF WORDS IS NEGLECTED

My book of words is neglected,
The boys are asking me why –
Why don't I write a new poem,
So I reply with a sigh –
'Jerry' is rather a nuisance,
Calling upon us each night,
Fetching us all from our beds –
I feel too weary to write.
Oh that the 'jerries' slept their last sleep,
Fathoms down in the sea so deep!

[31]

I THINK THE HOOTING OF AN OWL

I think the hooting of an owl
Weird enough one's blood to freeze;
Or on a dark and stormy night,
Wind whistling through the trees.

A wee mouse nibbling at the floor,
Will cause a little alarm,
As wakened suddenly from sleep,
We fear we may come to harm.

Here's another eerie thing,
It once did happen to me;
Walking along a lonely road,
Something was walking with me.
'Twas on a dark drear winter's night –
A hedge between road and field,
Footsteps were keeping pace with me,
And oh, how I could have squealed!

Together, we went on and on,
And my nerves were all on edge,
As I listened to the rustle,
The other side of the hedge.

At last that stretch of road was done,
And I – I felt almost dead,
Then over the gate at the top,
There appeared a horse's head!

And many more uncanny sounds
There are, that will give us fright,
But surely the most weird of all,
Is sirens screeching in the night!

WHAT DID YOU FEEL LIKE, PILOT BOLD

What did you feel like, pilot bold,
When baling from your plane?
Did you think you would never land,
You would never see home again?

Dropping, dropping from the skies,
Into the lake you landed;
Wet and clinging to a boat,
You were completely stranded.

A queer sensation it would be,
Such a ducking you got, too,
Then an angry keeper told you
How to paddle your canoe!

The penalty you could receive,
For putting the ducks to flight;
And never once enquiring
How you came in such a plight!

O MAN, WHAT SAY YOU TO THE NEWS?

O man, what say you to the news?
Your troubles will soon begin,
With short socks coming shorter,
How can you hold up your chin?

For yes, it is now decreed
They shall be five inches shorter;
Your wife will soon admonish you,
Like she does her son or daughter.

You will have to watch your step,
Keep your eye on them all the time;
'Pull 'em up,' she will gently say, -
And you – 'O hang those socks o' mine.'

You won't be on your dignity,
If you pull 'em up in the street,
And 'twill be less dignified still,
To let 'em dangle round your feet.

But there's a way to overcome,
This trouble with socks so small,
Take my advice, be like the girls,
And don't wear any at all!

O Sabbath bell, O Sabbath bell,
We long again to hear
Ringing through the silent air,
Your notes, so sweet and clear;
Your melodies, O Sabbath bell,
Spake of a peace divine,
But oh! 'tis long, so long ago,
Since last we heard you chime.

O Sabbath bell, we know one day,
Your chimes will come a-stealing.
Spreading happy echoes round,
With your merry pealing:
When wars are o'er, O Sabbath bell,
We will hear you again,
Telling us all with your sweet
                              chime,
Peace once again doth reign.

E·M·R

A page from the original journal

'TIS AUTUMN LATE, 'TIS AUTUMN LATE

'Tis autumn late, 'tis autumn late.
We see the fall of the leaf,
Everywhere the trees are bare,
Oh, why is summer so brief!

Thickly carpeted on the ground,
Lie these leaves of withered hue;
Summer's fled, and flowers are dead,
And autumn is nearly through.

The russet pears and apples,
Are gathered from the bough;
Hedgerows bare, where berries grow,
'Twill soon be winter now.

The playgrounds are neglected,
Where children's voices rang;
And tree tops are forsaken,
Where thrush and blackbird sang.

The days are dark and dreary,
Grey clouds o'ershadow the sky,
And gardens have been rifled,
With cold winds that whistle by.

Dead leaves and falling rain
Makes a scene so desolate;
Indoors, we seek for comforts,
Which will more than compensate.

The fire is burning brightly,
The cat on the rug does curl;
I sit in my easy chair,
My needles click knit and purl.

And the kettle on the hob
Is singing a song to me,
Such a cheery welcome sound -
And we'll have hot crumpets for tea!

'TWAS A DREARY NOVEMBER DAY

'Twas a dreary November day,
I was a long way from town,
Walking along a country road,
And the rain was tumbling down.

You'll guess how my heart was cheered
When a bus came along that road,
I took the only vacant seat;
The driver set off with his load.

I gazed on the dismal scene;
Sorry for those we passed by –
Oh how I thanked my lucky stars,
For having a seat in the dry!

We had not travelled very far,
When drip, drip, I heard, like a tap –
How did that small pool of water,
Ever come to be in my lap?

I was mystified at first,
Then all of a sudden the truth
Dawned on me – I looked above –
The rain came in through the roof!

DEAR ME, WHAT A WORLD IT IS!

Dear me, what a world it is!
So many good things we miss,
But all gloomy thoughts we'll dismiss,
And smile, smile, smile.
It's no good to whine and fret,
For the things we cannot get,
We've never gone hungry yet,
Be glad the while!

That little garden square,
Must not remain so bare,
Potatoes will grow there,
Get busy and dig.
In the kitchen we save peelings,
They will stave off hungry feelings,
And quieten the squealings
Of someone's pig!

It's no use looking at fashions,
Now clothes are among the 'rations,'
We've just got to curb our passions,
And 'make do' again.

Do we like it? - I doubt it
Though we can do well without it,
And to kick up a fuss about it
Is really insane!

That shirt must have another patch,
Even though the stuff won't match!
We cannot be right up to the scratch,
As before!
So toiling, patching or diggin',
Let there be no misgivin,'
We're promised a grand world to live in,
After the war!

Keep factory fires burning,
Though for rest we may be yearning,
See that the wheels keep turning,
And never cease!
Let not murm'rings cause delay,
Unite and toil for the happy day, -
Remember too that we must pray,
For lasting peace!

YELLOWING LEAVES

Yellowing leaves
A carpet weaves,
As autumn sheds her dress,
Faded and sere,
Strewn far and near,
What a litter and mess!

Busy we sweep
Them in a heap,
Toiling with patience and care;
And bonfires blaze –
A smoky haze
Fills the chill autumn air.

Hedgerows are kissed
With gossamer mist,
The blossoms all are dead;
Nights grow longer,
Winds blow stronger,
The golden glory has fled.

THE SUN SHONE BRIGHT, THE SKY WAS CLEAR

The sun shone bright, the sky was clear,
The day was so fair and warm,
The buds, the flowers were all so new,
On a beautiful April morn.

The countryside was calling me –
It struck to the very core –
I journeyed to the little cot,
Where oft I have gone before.

In peaceful solitude it stood,
And all around me glancing,
I thought I never had before,
Seen anything so entrancing.

The fruit trees were in blossom,
And, climbing the old cottage wall,
The pear tree that was blooming there,
In splendour, out-shone them all.

Hyacinths, primroses, daffies,
All growing so bright and gay,
And down the little garden path,
Forget-me-nots, paved the way.

Bewitched by the old-world charm,
I thought as I gazed before me,
Country life is sweet, so sweet; -
It cast a spell right o'er me.

Indoors I rested awhile,
Of refreshments, gladly partaking,
But ere my thirst was appeased,
I received a rude awak'ning!

Two cups of tea I had enjoyed,
While sipping through number three,
An amusing tale of little frogs,
Was being narrated to me.

Of how a butterfly net was made -
The fun in trying to capture
The little hopping creatures,
Was told in careless rapture.

Four of them lived deep down in a well,
As happy as happy could be;
But horrors! the water from that well,
Was used for my cup of tea!

I will not live in the country,
Where water is drawn from the well;
The little froggy incident,
Has broken the magic spell.

ANOTHER GREAT MILESTONE PASSED

Another great milestone passed!-
'Ere the leaves of autumn fall,
Italy, - Nazi satellite,
Has surrendered all!
Our gallant men have fought and toiled,
All through the weary years;
And now triumphant smiles replace
'The blood, the sweat and tears'.

Avenging hosts for freedom's cause,
Though travel-stained, weary and worn,
In this grim task, thrust forward,
To the glories of the morn;-
From Africa to Sicily,
Now marching on to Rome,-
The road still is hard and stony,
But 'tis the one that leads to home.

Victory bells and trumpets blare
Resound through-out our England home,
Proclaim with pride the glorious deeds,
Of those dear lads across the foam;-
For another milestone is passed,
Another great victory won,
Another step nearer to the goal,
And another grand job well done!

EASTER-TIDE – THE BELLS ARE RINGING

Easter-tide – the bells are ringing,
To proclaim that Christ is risen;
But what is that we also hear?
The sirens wailing – Listen!

Blessed Redeemer of the world,
He who died to save us,
He who suffered on the cross,
Life everlasting, gave us.

He is risen, He is risen,
The bells in triumph, proclaim;
We should be filled with joy and love ,
And praise his glorious name.

But lo! The other mournful sound
Whispers, 'No, it cannot be,
For from the fettered chains of war,
We still are praying to be free.'

The one, a gladsome message,
To all the world imparts,
The other bringing shades of doubt,
Which creep into our hearts.

Forgive us then if we despair,
When death from the sky is hurled,
Our faith is so severely tried,
In this topsy-turvy world.

IT WAS IN THE EARLY MORNING

It was in the early morning,
One a.m. to be correct,
Crackle! Pop, pop, pop, awoke us,
I drew the curtain to inspect.

There, just opposite, I saw
Flames, demoniac, shooting high,
Spurting venom far and wide,
Reflecting horror in the sky.

'Get up, get up,' I called to all,
Throw off your night attire,
Hurry, dress as quick as you can.
The gas works is on fire.'

'Twas thus I warned the household
That danger was right here,
We heard the fire bell clanging,
We saw the men draw near.

We, so helpless, wait and watch,
With anxious eyes and bated breath,
Can they check that blazing fire?
Can they curb those fangs of death?

With blistered hands, they ply the hose
On flames that the breezes fan,
An evil task – seems not human –
Too much to ask of mortal man.

But still they toil with sweated brow,
An anxious hour goes by; -
The flaming tongues seem not so fierce,
Less angry, seems the sky.

Yet another hour has passed, -
Their duties they never shun,
Their labour has not been in vain,
The battle with flames, is won.

The fire is spent, the ruins show
Just charred and twisted frames,
All is safe, give thanks and bless
The men who fought the flames;
For had those venom tongues but spread,
We might have numbered with the dead.

WHAT AILS THE CUCKOO IN THE CLOCK?

What ails the cuckoo in the clock?
He'll start to sing and then he'll stop;
He should come forward from his bower,
To tell each passing quarter hour.

On strike! – That's an unfounded fear,
He's served me well for many a year;
Perhaps he's weary, - I know he's old –
Maybe it's just a little cold.

A cold! That's it! He's lost his zest,
And needs a something to grease his chest,
For though he'll 'cuck', it's strange to say,
He hasn't 'oo'd for many a day.

BITTER THE NIGHT, AND OH, HOW IT SNOWS!

Bitter the night, and oh, how it snows!
Hark how the blustering North wind blows!
Now work is done, doors and windows make fast,
We're glad to shut out the cold wintry blast.

Stir the coals, make the flames leap higher,
Draw your chairs near to the welcome fire;
Round the hearth with our loved ones beside us,
We find a peace the world has denied us.

Last night I dreamed; - I'll relate it to you,
(I wish I could think it would soon come true)
I dreamt we lived in a beautiful land,
Everything plentiful, oh it was grand!

Fruitful orchards, and pastures so green,
Rich golden corn, in abundance was seen,
Gardens where flowers in profusion did bloom,
Not anywhere was there a shadow of gloom.

A pennon waved from a high Church steeple,
I saw a multitude of people; -
Men, women and children, ten thousand strong,
A joyous excited eager throng.

An organ swelled with a glad refrain,
Choristers sang it, again and again,
It was 'Peace on earth, goodwill to men,'
And echoing voices sang 'Amen'.

Guns were all silenced, and strife was o'er;
Dear ones returned to part never more,
Sheathed was the gleaming sword's cruel blade,
Heads were uplifted, none shrank back afraid.

The joy of the people remains so clear,
The choristers' song, I still can hear;
There was 'Peace on earth, goodwill to men,'
When will my dream come true – oh when?

JUST AT THE FOOT OF DIXTON HILL

Just at the foot of Dixton Hill,
A picturesque cottage stands,
As far as the eye can see around,
There are pleasant green pasture lands.

In lonely solitude, there it's been,
For a hundred years or more,
Happy the hours I have spent there,
But alas! I will go no more.

For years I've been to that cottage,
It almost seemed part of my life;
I've felt the warm zephyr breezes,
And winds that have cut like a knife.

And sometimes, in my childhood days,
I would stay the whole summer through,
Now memories only are left me,
I can scarcely believe it's true.

I would roam the orchard at will,
'Neath the heavily laden boughs;
I would pause by the gate in the hedge,
To watch the sheep as they browse.

I would laze in the garden fair,
Beneath a clear summer sky;
And my heart would swell with joy,
When the lark sang his paeons on high.

And from that old-world garden,
I'd cull many a fragrant bloom,
As from the distance there would come
The sound of the wood doves' croon.

We'd have tea in a cosy room,
(In days gone by a dairy) –
We'd chat and laugh the hours away
Just me and my Aunt Mary.

And through the lattice window,
Came the humming of the bees,
And the perfume of the roses,
Floated sweetly with the breeze.

Robin would come through the open door –
A cheeky young rascal was he –
He would hop all over the table,
The while we were having tea.

And plain fare, - he just simply scorned,
He helped himself freely to cake,
He'd pick sultanas from our hands,
And e'en from our lips would take.

And if, in my travels I go that way,
The cottage I'll pass with a sigh,
For the doors are all closed against me,
And this is the reason why: -

There is no one there to greet me
With a kiss of fond affection,
The open arms, the welcome smile,
Afford sweet recollection.

Life's journey for her, is over;
In the churchyard she lies sleeping;
The troubled world disturbs her not,
We've left her in God's safe keeping.

HERE WE STAND AT THE ALERT

Here we stand at the alert,
Waiting for the final spurt;
This experience is not new,
Four years ago, remember you? –
There was a similar occasion,
When we awaited an invasion.

But now, how different! Yes, 'tis so,
'Tis we who wait the signal, 'Go,'
All day, all night, the planes they roar,
Winging a way to the invasion shore,
Paving the way for those who'll brave,
The shot and shell and the angry wave.

Friends who are waiting over there,
Will readily of the burden share,
And weary tho' the waiting be,
The day will dawn when they'll be free; -
Tho' many the hardships that entail,
We must not, DARE NOT, SHALL NOT fail.

I'M FED UP! – I REALLY AM!

I'm fed up! – I really am!
I'm sick of margarine and jam,
I'd like some butter, thickly spread,
On a nice wafer of new, white bread; -
What wouldn't I give for peaches and cream,
And wouldn't I mop my dish up clean!
A rich cream puff, or a chocolate éclair,
Would help to sweeten the meagre fare; -
And what can one do with two ounces of cheese?
(Oh, give us a bigger ration, please),
And a tender steak would be nice, of course, -
I could swear sometimes we're eating horse; -
Bananas and nuts are quite 'taboo,'
And oranges, well they're far too few! –
Here's just a little of what we've missed,
And somehow or other we still exist!
And what is more we're better forsooth,
That's what we're told, so I suppose it's the truth, -
But give me, oh give me the chance to pick,
I'd have them again and risk being sick.

'I'VE HAD SUCH A NARROW ESCAPE,'

'I've had such a narrow escape,'
Said a mouse to her children one day,
'I was hunting for food and found some,
'On a gas stove, not far away.'

'Someone's dinner, it did smell good,
'I wanted to burst into song;
'I ran up the stove to help myself,
'But my dears, I stayed too long.'

'Some fiends – I think they're called "boys,"
'Espied me , - I had to be quick, -
'They yelled with delight while trying
'To poke my ribs with a stick.'

'At last I heard one of them say,
'We'll be late for school, come hurry,
'Now I don't know what a school is,
'But I felt I need not worry.'

'And so for a while, I lay low,
'To recover from my fright,
'Until at last no sound was heard,
'And thought to venture forth I might.'

'I peeped out from my hiding place,
'A sight sent my heart pit-a-pat;
'For looking up with glaring eyes,
'Was a horrible beast of a cat!'

'And there I stayed, for hours it seemed,
'So scared and still as the dead;
'Till puss at last got weary,
'And then I just simply fled.'

'But I'll have my revenge one day,
'I'll nibble and scratch all the paint,
'And now my dears, I must rest,
'For I'm really feeling quite faint.'

OLD MAN WINTER

Old man Winter, you're hard and you're cruel,
You know we've been ordered to go easy with fuel,
Yet you come along in your gripping might,
And deeper than ever is your cutting bite.

I'll say I admire your elegant grace,
As the fairy like ferns on my window I trace;
What magic enchantment your artist'ry weaves,
Such crystal-clear icicles hang from the eaves.

All the trees are adorned with a lacy design,
Of purest white - exquisitely fine,
The frost-bound brook, every wee blade of grass,
Escapes not your glittering spear as you pass.

All seems a fairyland - dazzling white,
But some of your deeds are as black as night
King of the Ice, oh haven't you revelled,
At treacherous deeds where your spear has levelled!

The water tap's frozen, the milk's frozen too,
The cistern is cracked, - but what's that to you?
There's a burst at the main, I shudder, oh lor;
As I think of the mess, when along comes the thaw!

The roads are so slithery, shiny as glass,
You laugh with delight - you're an ignorant ass -
When one goes down with such mighty force, -
- Now that sense of humour is vulgar and coarse!

Perhaps in the past, in some certain measure,
I did think you fun, I did derive pleasure,
But now it is different, your coldness intense,
Gnaws through to the bone, and numbs every sense.

I just want to sit, and thaw by the fire,
I'd so like to heap it, higher and higher,
But we're rationed, yes RATIONED for all our fuel,
Old man, old man, indeed you are cruel!

APRIL 23RD, 1945

Mark it well, - tonight, tonight
We walk from darkness into light, -
A symbol of triumph, victory near,
Of a precious freedom we all hold dear. -
In suburban street and city square
Twinkling lights are everywhere,
No sirens feared, no terror, dread
Of approaching horrors overhead;
The fearful drone of death is gone,
Hurrah! Hurray! the lights are on!

MAY 8TH, 1945

Happy day, oh glorious day,
With bunting, flags, we've all gone gay,
Work is forgotten, care brushed aside,
High exultation reigns far and wide.

Pent-up emotions of war-weary years,
Burst wild and free, with laughter and cheers,
Mingled with strains from the singing throng,
Voices upraised in a thanksgiving song.

And kiddies, among bomb-scarred ruins, dance,
To the ear-splitting music of old tin cans,
Blaring trumpets - "musical" toys,
Anything - ANYTHING, - that makes a noise.

Chiming bells in triumphant voice,
Merrily say, 'Rejoice, rejoice';
And hark to the birds, they carol so gay,
Do they know too that it's VE day?

Incidentally, it is my natal day,
So *I* rejoice in a two-fold way,
And of all my presents, large and small,
THIS IS THE VERY BEST GIFT OF ALL.

COMIC PAPERS – WHAT PRICELESS JOY, -

Comic papers – what priceless joy, -
More precious than any expensive toy! –
Don't the youngsters just love them handy –
The 'Knock-out', 'the Beano', 'Film Fun', or the 'Dandy'.

Silence reigns as the pages they turn,
The adventures of 'Desperate Dan' to learn,
And aren't they just eager to read of the fate
Of that young nosey-parker, sly 'Key-hole Kate',
Of 'Lazy Larry', (the idle old rotter)
'Tin-can Tommy', and 'Pansy Potter',
Likewise 'Our Gang' – the laughter is loud –
They delight to mix up with that silly crowd;
With 'Eggo' the ostrich, and 'Korky', the cat,
'Cutlass', the captain, so ugly and fat,
The school m'arm 'Ma Murphy' and sweet 'Little Nell',
Not forgetting that friend of hers; wise 'Peter Pell',
'Chutney' too, the notorious cook,
And greedy old 'Horace', with the hungry look,
Also bright 'Marvo', and 'Freddie', the fly,
The hours slip quietly, pleasantly by.

Comic papers, something to prize,
Something the youth in his teens won't despise,
The toddler, the schoolboy and – yes, it is true –
But I'll whisper it softly, - father too!

I'VE JUST HAD SUCH A SHOCK

I've just had such a shock,
I nearly jumped off my feet,
I opened the oven door,
And a mouse ran off the meat;
And dinner is at one,
But my appetite is gone!

AUG 14th, 1945.

Peace has come to all the world,
Banners are again unfurled,
Hopes are high and spirits gay,
It's come, it's here, it's V.J. day!

Doors are opened, neighbours call,
'Hear the news?' asks one and all;
'The war is over,' and so it's spread,
And awakens many a sleepy head.

Out in the street, they congregate,
And excitedly plan, 'though the hour is late;
Young folk too, have their own ideas,
With noisy prattle and rousing cheers,
On through the streets they go their way,
Light-heartedly they swing and sway,
Greeting a pal with, 'Hello, what cheer!
Come along with us, my dear.'

Trees illumined in the 'Prom,'
Draw the crowd magnetically on,
Dancing here – a 'show' staged there,
Jostling together, devil-may-care,
Trumpets, streamers, waving flags,
Music, fireworks, student 'rags',
'Tis thus, - the exuberance of youth,
(Wild revellers in very truth)
In carnival dress and cap complete,
Bring gaiety, colour to every street,
They shout and laugh with all their might,
And dance and sing throughout the night;
But see! The older generation,
Seek quiet meditation;
With thankful hearts they kneel and pray,
Pray that peace has come to stay;
But gay or solemn be the mood,
All hearts are filled with gratitude,
Joyous in this glad release,
God grant it be a *lasting* peace.

I'M OFF TO SHEFFIELD, I AWAIT MY TRAIN

I'm off to Sheffield, I await my train,
I'm off to the old home town again,
I'm going to see the people I know,
'Tis long since we met, 'tis six years ago.

An interesting place is a railway station,
It has for me a strange fascination –
The trains steaming in, and then steaming out,
The porters all busy, bustling about,
Pulling their trolleys with luggage piled high,
Mixed up in the crowd, striving hard to get by,
The conversations reaching the ear,
'Pleasant journey,' – 'Send a line, my dear,' –
'Call on the old folks,' – 'My love to Sue,' –
But it's 3.15 and our train is now due.
Here she comes, - It's ours I guess –
Round the bend, the Sheffield express,
Puffing, snorting, majestically proud,
Ready to pick up this jolly old crowd.
Affectionate partings, more hurried farewells,
The crowd on the platform suddenly swells
As people alight from the incoming train,
And others just struggle to get on the same.
Phew! What a struggle for a seat,
(A youngster delights to stand on my feet),
And now we're all settled, happy and gay,
The guard blows his whistle. We're off and away.

*   *   *   *   *   *

We're speeding along, we've travelled far,
We are many miles from Cheltenham Spa;
From Birmingham, Burton, Derby we fly,
And Chesterfield's crooked steeple we spy.
We arouse ourselves, we take notice here,
For the end of our journey is drawing near,

Through Totley tunnel, by Millhouses Park,
And we will arrive before it is dark.

*   *   *   *   *   *

Well, here we are at our destination,
Is this it? – What devastation!
Where are the shops I knew of old,
The windows that glittered with silver and gold,
The scented florists, with blooms so gay,
I would pause to admire when I went that way.
The windows of fashion I still recall,
The music, the bookshops, where are they all?

*   *   *   *   *   *

Here they lie, those shops of old,
Here they lie, just rubble and mould,
Shattered and scattered by war's cruel blow,
('Mid some of the ruins, wild flowers now grow),
A twisted frame here – there charred wood
May still mask a place where some building stood;
Oh; the destruction, the heartaches, the sighs –
But a grand new city never-the-less will rise,
For wars are over, fluttering high
Victory's banners proudly fly;
Some day instead of rubble and mould,
New streets, new shops, will replace the old.

LADIES, DEAR LADIES, AUSTERITY GOES

Ladies, dear ladies, austerity goes,
Here is the latest about your new clothes,
Restrictions are lifted and you may now grace,
Your 'undies' with ribbon, embroidery, lace!
Tucks in your blouses, pleats in your skirts, -
And you gentlemen – longer tails to your shirts,
'Turn ups' on trousers and your wretched socks,
From now shall be lengthened and brightened with 'clocks.'

Nighties of 'nylon,' with delicate smockings, -
In the shops once again, full-fashioned stockings;
Ruflettes so dainty your neck will adorn,
Flounces and flares on your dress may be worn,
The shortage of pockets that you did deplore, -
Well, you may have them, and belts once more,
And buttons in plenty, - all you desire;
And now, here's a cheer for Staff Cripps, Esquire.

LIFE IS SO DIFFICULT, WHY, OH WHY?

Life is so difficult, why, oh why?
It makes me weary, it makes me sigh.
War has been over for a whole long year
But there's little enough to bid us cheer.
Houses are wanted, but oh, what a hope,
There's less cheese, less fats, less beer, less soap;
We've suffered long with the meagre fare,
Of meatless days we've had our share,
Now comes an order that we really dread,
For we must be rationed for our daily bread.
It's points for this and points for that,
Coupons for clothing, - I've got it off "pat",
But these BU's*! I'll never get wise
To the "B.U.X's" and the "B.U.Y's"
The "L" and the "M", and the "G" and the "J",
I'm thinking it out and struggling all day.
I puzzle and puzzle, but all in vain,
I *still* cannot get it fixed in my brain.

*B.U's - Bread units.

HOLIDAY TIME COMES ROUND ONCE MORE

Holiday time comes round once more,
This time for me it's the breezy shore;
The train set off with a puff and a screech,
A few hours later, I lazed on the beach.

*   *   *   *   *   *

The sky is blue, so very blue,
Its reflection falls on the water too;
The wavelets dance so light and free,
And a gentle wind blows in from the sea.

'Tis pleasant to idle the hours away,
Watching the children at their play,
Light of heart, healthy and tanned,
Eagerly building their castles of sand,
Or frolicking near the water's tip,
While some, more venturesome, take a dip,

Maybe a steamer trip, you crave,
Or just a small pleasure boat riding a wave,
A 'Try your skill,' the fair, the pier,
Attractions in plenty, but I'm staying here,
For I have to feel that breeze kissing me,
As it comes, oh so gently, over the sea.

How lovely it is! How serenely calm!
It offers healing, strength and balm;
The tide comes in; the modest waves,
Silently fill the inlets and caves.

But 'tis not always so. Now yesterday
The clouds hung heavy, the skies were grey,
The soft wind awoke and soon got stirring,
The waves, no longer gently purring,
Arose; we heard the voice of the sea,
And knew how angry and wild it could be.

We watched in wonder from the 'Prom',
Watched the waves come sweeping on
With stormy wrath. The incoming tide
Tossed its volumes far and wide
In a maddening rush, as if overdue –
The thunderous roar drowned the seagulls' mew, -
Grasping all it could in that blundering chase,
And holding it fast in its cruel embrace
With possessive might. Its grandeur appals,
As each giant wave leaps higher then falls,
Only to tumble and rollick and roll,
On and on, till it reaches its goal,
The sea wall – even so its fury to vent,
Still not weary, nor yet spent,
And leaping high towards us dashing,
Made us run to escape a splashing;
Roaring aloud in spirited glee,
At the madcap adventures of the mighty sea.

SORROW HAS COME TO ME, GRIEF AND DESPAIR

Sorrow has come to me, grief and despair,
My heart is heavy, the cross hard to bear;
So cruelly sudden came that midnight call,
That took my beloved, my dearest of all.

All in a moment, and there he lay, -
'A beautiful death', they one and all say –
But what of me so abruptly bereft? –
God help me, – the one that is left.

THE LAGGING WEEKS PASS INTO MONTHS

The lagging weeks pass into months,
My heart echoes many a sigh,
My thoughts return again and again,
To those happy days gone by.

The future seemed rosy, secure; -
We talked of the house of our dreams,
And planned a beautiful garden, -
How far away it seems!

No cloud upon our household,
Only happiness reigned there,
Till death shattered all, and now life is
So empty, so barren, so bare.

No partner to share life's journey,
Hope gone, no interest I crave;
There's only a garden I cherish,
Just one little plot, - his grave.

WELL MY BOYS, MY BOOK IS DONE

Well my boys, my book is done,
I will not write another,
P'raps as you read it, through the years,
You'll spare a thought for MOTHER.

It grieves me that the final brings
No 'happy ever' magic,
How could I know, how could I dream,
It would all end up so tragic?

Dec. 1947.